WHERE DID I
COME FROM?

WHERE DID I
COME FROM?

*A Guide for Parents on Science, Evolution,
Human Origins, and the Christian Faith*

Rev. James Bradley Miller, PhD

CONTENTS

ACKNOWLEDGMENTS

No author can produce a resource such as this without significant support. First and foremost I am grateful to my wife, Kathleen Calder Miller, who for more than 50 years has indulged my eccentric, quasi-career in a marginal, if not imaginary, field and has steadfastly and persistently encouraged my completion of this work.

Local congregations reviewed early drafts. Their comments and suggestions were invaluable in the refinement not only of the text, but the general organization and format of the resource. While not all of these reviewers provided their names during the review process, I want to particularly express my gratitude to these people for their insights: Chris Abel, Sharon Miller Cindrich, Rev. Donald O. and Ann R. Clendaniel, Bill Cook, James P. Deaver, Nordia Dixon, Kristin Dounian, Ande I. Emmanuel, Charles W. Johnson Jr., Carole Lee, David Lord, Tea Madden, John Monroe, Henry Rivers, Sam Rivers, James Sawers, Roberta L. Shepard, Laura Stratton, Miller White, Jane Williams, and Lisa Preis Wong.

This resource is the outgrowth of the work of the Broader Social Impacts Committee of the Human Origins Program of the Smithsonian Institution's National Museum of Natural History. I am indebted to my fellow committee members for their encouragement: Francisca Cho, Eliott Dorff, Fred Edwords, Betty Holley, Nancy Howell, Randy Isaac, Wes McCoy, Mustansir Mir, Ravi Ravindra, Wentzel Van Huyssteen, Joe Watkins, and Fr. Tom Weinandy. I am especially grateful to my co-chair of that committee, Connie Bertka, for her ever-constructive suggestions on all aspects of this writing project.

Staff of the Smithsonian's Human Origins Program have helped bring this effort to fruition. Paleoanthropologist, Briana Pobiner, has helped me understand how human evolution is continuing. Museum specialist, Jennifer Clark, was crucially instrumental in gaining me permission to use the compelling hominin illustrations in this work.

Lastly, but primarily, I am grateful for the vision, perseverance, and insight of Rick Potts, director of the Smithsonian's Human Origins Initiative and curator of the David H. Koch Hall of Human Origins of the National Museum of Natural History. His appreciation of the rich cultural complexity of the science and religion relationship, his patient scientific tutoring, his collegiality, and most importantly, his friendship, provided invaluable encouragement to this most difficult task of preparing an educational resource on science and religion accessible to members of local congregations.

In all of this it is truly the case that, as Isaac Newton declared, "I stand on the shoulders of giants."

INTRODUCTION

"Daddy, where did I come from?" asked eight-year-old Diana one evening while she and her father were reviewing her homework. Somewhat embarrassed, her father, Jack, offered a rambling account of human biology and procreation. When he paused for a moment to catch his breath, Diana said, "That's all very interesting, Daddy, but what I really wanted to know was whether I came from Cleveland or Pittsburgh."

Of course, Diana might as easily have said, "Daddy, what I really wanted to know was whether I came from Adam and Eve or a monkey." Children are infinitely curious, and questions about our origins, both as persons and as a species, are probably as old as humankind itself and were a subject around ancient campfires.

Parents are on the front line of children's curiosity. A child's persistent "Why?" can drive a parent to distraction. But children's questions emerge from their wonder of the world around them. They experience plants and animals, the changing seasons, the sun and moon, and the myriads of stars at night. They experience family, school, and church. They experience a wide range of media, from galleries and museums, to books and television, and an increasing number of social media. The total experiential input for children today is staggering. At the same time, children are cognitive sponges that are capable of absorbing huge amounts of information. Yet, there are few places in their or our lives where such diverse information is brought together as a whole, in a comprehensive and coherent manner.

This is a resource for adults. In particular, though not exclusively, it is a resource for parents in Christian congregations. The primary purpose of this resource is to help Christian parents better address questions that their children may have about the relationship between Christian and scientific accounts of nature, of the origin of human beings, and of the place of humans in nature.

In Sunday school and church, children learn traditional Bible stories about God as creator, Adam and Eve, and human responsibility in relation to the rest of creation. In school and in science-based television shows, they learn about the evolution of the universe and life, the biological kinship of all living things, and the ecological interdependence of life on Earth. These two sets of learning experiences do not necessarily conflict, but it is not self-evident how they fit together. The purpose of this resource is to suggest ways that parents can help provide their children with a coherent understanding of their place in nature as creations of God.

This resource addresses six questions. It is designed for flexible use either in adult church school settings with parents, or by parents exploring these questions on their own at home. In church school settings, the sessions can be used in a six-part series, in a three-part series of two questions each, or in a two-part series of three questions each, depending on available time or place for its use in the life of the congregation.

But the resource also could serve as a general resource for parents as they anticipate questions that could emerge at home in ordinary conversations they have with their children. This resource also might serve parents who have chosen to home school their children.

Each chapter of the resource has been written to be both concise and accessible. Over the past fifty years, there has been a veritable explosion of academic writing on science and religion. This resource is not intended to be an academic tome. At the same time, the reader may be curious about some of the subject matter and would like more information. So, at the end of this guide are some suggested resources that provide more in-depth discussion of the science, history, and theology that are introduced throughout the guide in a more summary fashion.

In addition, there is a closing section of this resource titled, **"More of the Story…"** This section is like an expanded glossary that includes definitions, brief biographical notes, or short elaborations of topics identified in **red** throughout the main body of this resource.

The first question is not actually one that children are likely to ask. This is the question about *the relationship between religious traditions about creation and scientific discoveries about nature.* Parents' understanding of this question and their answer to it sets the framework within which all the other particular questions about Christian faith and science will be addressed.

The second question might well come from a child who has watched a show about primates on Animal Planet on a Sunday afternoon. Did we come from apes or Adam and Eve? What is humanity's place in the tree of life? *Does the scientific account of human origins contradict the traditional Genesis accounts of the creation of the first humans?* Must children choose between the Bible and science?

The third question is closely related to the second. The Bible—and frequently preachers—speaks of humans as "made in the image of God." But the scientific account of the evolution of *Homo sapiens* shows a many-stage emergence of the features that are distinctive in or unique to human beings. *What is "the image of God?"* Does it set humans off in a fundamental way from all other creatures? Does it imply a degree of privilege within the order of nature?

Are humans the product of a plan or the outcome of happenstance? This is **the fourth question.** Are human beings necessary in the history of nature or are they the result of the accidental convergence of a wide variety of natural processes? The biblical traditions focus the drama of creation around the story of human beings. On the other hand, evolutionary processes are contingent; that is, the natural history of Earth could have worked out differently, without *Homo sapiens*. What is the ultimate or religious status of human beings, if their appearance as a species was only a probability and not a certainty?

And what about all the death along the way? Plants die, animals die, human beings die, and the path of the evolution of life on Earth is strewn with the carcasses of a countless number of species that have become extinct. Death and suffering brought on by natural disasters have perennially been a challenge for the Christian belief in a good Creator. The monumental carnage of the processes of evolution only magnifies this challenge. ***So, the fifth question addresses the problem of "natural evil."***

Paleontologists report that there have been five massive extinction events in the history of the Earth and we may be in the midst of a sixth. What distinguishes this sixth is that humans are a significant cause of it. The evolutionary impact of human beings—the proliferation of *Homo sapiens* across the whole surface of the Earth and the impact of this biological explosion on the habitats of other species and the global ecology—is perhaps only rivaled in the history of life by the evolution of oxygen-producing, photosynthetic life forms. The Bible speaks of humans as both dominators of creation and as caretakers. ***How does the scientific account of the origin and evolution of* Homo sapiens *cast light on traditional pictures of humanity's place in the scheme of life on Earth.*** This is **the sixth question** to be considered.

The authority of the Bible is a final matter that must be considered in this introduction. It is a topic that lies behind each of the questions considered here. This resource assumes the most common position of Christians regarding the books that together comprise the Old and New Testaments. That position is that these texts are a unique and necessary witness to God and an infallible guide to the beliefs and practices of the Christian community.

At the same time, it is obvious that all Christians do not share a common understanding of what these texts mean because the Christian family has so many branches. The texts of the Bible always require interpretation. Even the

Bible itself illustrates this requirement where texts from the Old Testament are interpreted in the New.

This resource assumes an early and traditional Christian understanding of the Bible and its language; namely, that the texts were composed using forms of expression and ideas that fit the ways of thinking common to its readers or those who heard it read. So, for example, God is often referred to in monarchial rather than in democratic language (as king rather than president) because that was the most common form of political organization in the ancient world of the Middle East.

Given the need for Biblical interpretation, this resource assumes that God has provided four sources that together contribute to an authoritative religious understanding of God and God's creation: the Biblical texts, the reader's experience of creation itself, the gift of reason that helps refine an understanding of God and the meaning of creation, and the historical tradition of the Christian community as it has sought throughout various ages to discern God and God's creation.

Discussion Questions

1 Have your children ever asked you questions like those posed in this resource? If so, did you feel as though you were well equipped to answer them?

2 Have you yourself ever wondered about these questions? If so, were there opportunities in your congregation to discuss such questions?

3 Has your minister preached on any of these questions?

4 Are there other questions about science, evolution, human origins, and the Christian faith that your children have asked? Are there other such questions that you have wondered about? Make a list of those for possible future study and discussion.

5 What does the expression, "the authority of the Bible," mean to you? Can you think of examples of how your personal experience of creation, your reasoning, and/or your understanding of church traditions have contributed to your understanding of the Bible?

I

Competitors, Acquaintances, or Companions

"I don't get it, Liz. Here is another report in the paper about controversy in a school district over teaching evolution. Sure, there have been conflicts in the past, but aren't science and religion basically different things? I mean if they deal with different questions and have different methods, how can they conflict? What is there to argue about?"

"Well, you know, Jack, Pastor Mike seemed to agree with you in his sermon last week. He was talking about science and religion being two ways of knowing that are different but complementary," Liz answered. "But, then I started wondering, if they are so separate, why do some religious people seem to think that science challenges their beliefs? I have to say that sometimes I wonder if we live in one world on Sunday and another the other six days of the week."

Underlying all the following sections of this resource is the basic question of the relationship between science and Christianity. Public discussions of this relationship commonly use adversarial language like "debate." Some people see science and Christianity as all out competitors. They assume that people must choose to give their allegiance to one or the other.

On the other hand, when asked personally, many Americans say they see no conflict between science and Christianity because each deals with different matters and has its own separate domain of authority. Here, science and Christianity are seen as acquaintances. They recognize each other but are not intimately related.

A third view has been developing over the past three quarters of a century. A growing number of religious scholars and scientists see the relationship as one of historical interaction, with science and Christianity influencing each other. In this view, science and Christianity are historical companions, each bearing upon the other, though perhaps in different ways.

All three of these positions point to events in western history for support.

Case One – Competitors: For the competitive view, there are two trials that are icons for the relationship of science and Christianity: **the trial of Galileo** before the Inquisition in seventeenth-century Rome, and the controversies surrounding Charles Darwin's *Origin of Species*, especially the so-called **Scopes Monkey Trial** in twentieth-century Dayton, Tennessee.

Galileo Galilei
1564-1642

Galileo before the Roman Inquisition, 1633

Thomas Scopes
1900-1970

Clarence Darrow cross exams
William Jennings Bryan, 20 July 1925

Certainly, a trial as an adversarial process is a form of conflict, but both of these trials involved issues well beyond science or Christianity as such. These two trials are the most common reference points for those who see an inevitable conflict between scientific inquiry and Christian tradition. But renewed historical study of these events has shown that they were much more complex than simple clashes between scientific explorers and religious traditionalists.

Case Two – Acquaintances: The acquaintance view of the relationship between science and Christianity was formed in large part from the works of two major western philosophers in the seventeenth and eighteenth centuries: **Rene Descartes**, often called the "father of modern philosophy," and **Immanuel Kant**.

Rene Descartes
1596-1650

Immanuel Kant
1724-1804

Pope John Paul II
1920-2005

Stephen Jay Gould
1941-2002

Taken together, Descartes and Kant gave initial voice to what has sometimes been called the "Kantian Truce" between science and religion. Science and religion could be friendly acquaintances without interfering with each other.

Today, this view is perhaps the most common and most popular among both religious leaders and many scientists. For example, **Pope John Paul II** and paleontologist, **Stephen Jay Gould**, shared the view that science and religion deal with different subjects.

Case Three – Companions: The idea that science and Christianity may be more interactive companions is not new. **Nicolas Copernicus** is often credited with initiating the modern scientific "revolution" when his *De revolutionibus orbium coelestium (On the Revolutions of the Celestial Orbs)* was published in 1543. Not only was he a mathematician, astronomer, and economic advisor to the King of Poland, but he was also a church administrator. He saw his study of the motions of the heavens as a religious act.

Augustine of Hippo
354-430 CE

Copernicus thought Christians have a religious reason for the scientific study of nature. Such study is not merely a religiously legitimate occupation. It is a fitting form of worship.

But centuries earlier, Christians were warned that they should be cautious about what they say about nature that might undermine the relationship between the Christian faith and the science of the day. **Augustine of Hippo** was one of the most influential early Christian theologians engaging classical western thought. He suggested that there are sometimes tensions between what can be reliably understood about nature and what some Christians want to claim the Bible says.

At very least, Augustine, a champion of scriptural authority, understood that there are occasions when tensions in the relationship between reliable scientific accounts of nature and the scriptural depictions of nature have to be resolved in favor of science, if science and the Christian faith are to remain companions.

Teilhard de Chardin, SJ
1881-1955

Much more recently, a Christian who was also a scientist, the Jesuit paleontologist, **Pierre Teilhard de Chardin**, expressed the challenge of sustaining such companionship. He affirmed that the understanding of a coherent relationship between science and religion is essential for personal and religious integrity in our day.

These three Christian voices point to a sort of companionship in which there is genuine sharing that makes a difference to each of the partners. In the case of Copernicus, scientific study of nature is encouraged as a form of Christian worship. Augustine implies that there can be no conflict between scientific understanding of nature and a biblical understanding of creation, and for Christians to claim such is a grievous error. Teilhard points to the need for a constantly renewing coherence between science and Christianity as new discoveries about God's creation are made. These voices clearly do not suggest that there is no difference between science and religion. Science and religion are not the same. But their differences neither separate nor isolate them from each other, much less place them in opposition.

Two more twentieth-century figures, **Albert Einstein** and **Holmes Rolston**, have captured in brief words the complexity of a mutually influential relationship of companionship between science and religion. Einstein wrote, "Science without religion is blind, religion without science is lame." In Rolston's words, "Religion that is married to science today will be a widow tomorrow…and religion that is divorced from science today will leave no offspring tomorrow."

But in concrete terms, how can science and religion interact

Albert Einstein
1889-1955

Holmes Rolston III
1932-present

today, particularly the sciences of human origins and Christianity? To begin, what might Christianity contribute to the science of human origins?

Mystery: Christianity can remind science that its most assured discoveries float upon a sea of mystery. Scientists themselves are aware of the deep mystery of nature. As evolutionary pioneer **J. B. S. Haldane** noted in 1927, "Now, my own suspicion is that the universe is not only queerer than we suppose, but queerer than we can suppose."

J.B.S. Haldane
1892-1964

In many ways, each new discovery about human origins or in any other science deepens our appreciation of what we do not know. Christianity reinforces humility as a scientific virtue.

Freedom and Responsibility: Christianity also reminds science that its endeavor is liberating: "…and you will know the truth, and the truth will make you free." (John 8:32) But genuine freedom also entails responsibility. The scientific enterprise is not value neutral. It always has an impact on the quality of life that humans experience. Because knowledge is power, Christianity also reminds science that the development and exercise of scientific knowledge is ethically and morally significant.

So, Christianity can contribute a framework of meaning and an ethical and moral perspective within which science can flourish. But, what can science, especially the sciences of human origins, contribute to Christianity?

Kinship: The sciences of human origins help Christians appreciate that they are both part of and participants in a creative process that is still ongoing. The sciences remind Christians that they are biologically linked with all other life forms on Earth as relatives. Life on Earth may be like a tree, but it is also profoundly a family. The sciences of human origins can help deepen a Christian's appreciation of the distinctive or unique features we bear as gifts of a creative evolutionary process. It can also remind Christians of human responsibilities in relation to all other life, our kin, which come from those gifts.

Alfred North-Whitehead
1861-1947

Our Challenge: Still, it is a challenge to determine how we will relate science and the Christian faith for our children and ourselves. In the early-twentieth-century, philosopher **Alfred North Whitehead** described the challenge in these terms, "When we consider what religion is for mankind, and what science is, it is no exaggeration to say that the future course of history depends upon the decision of this generation as to the relations between them."

The three options described briefly above can be found in America today. Like Jack and Liz, many Christians do not understand why science and religion are pitted against each other as competitors. But at the same time, they are unclear how to relate science and Christianity as more than mere acquaintances. This resource has been developed under the conviction that companionship is the most historically accurate, appropriate, and fruitful approach to the relationship for both science and Christianity. This is not to say that companions cannot argue from time to time or even go their separate ways for a while. However, it is the purpose of this resource to encourage companionship for today and in future generations. As such, the answers in the concluding narratives of each of the chapters are not **THE** answers to the questions posed by the opening narratives, but are answers that attempt to illustrate possible hard-won fruits of real companionship.

"You know, Jack," said Liz. "I think there are other parents in our church who also wonder about these things. Maybe we could get Pastor Mike to help us organize a discussion group that could think and talk about these kinds of questions together."

"That sounds like a good idea," responded Jack. "And, you know, we might also talk about how we can respond to our kids when they ask us questions about our Christian faith and the understanding of nature that science produces."

Discussion Questions

1 In your experience, what are some examples of science and Christianity as competitors?

2 In your experience, what are some examples of science and Christianity as aquaintances?

3 In your experience, what are some examples of science and Christianity relating to each other as companions?

4 What do you think some of the challenges are for science and for Christianity if their relationship is one of companionship?

5 If your child asked you if they had to choose between a scientific understanding of nature and a Christian understanding of creation, how would you respond?

6 Read the quote from Copernicus in "More of the Story." What do you think he meant when he declared, "…ignorance can not be more grateful than knowledge"? What might this suggest about a Christian's attitude toward science?

7 Read the quote from Augustine in "More of the Story." Can you think of examples in which some Christians have made claims about nature that cause non-Christians to be dismissive of the Christian faith as foolishness?

II

Adam and Lucy?

"Mom, I don't get it," Will exclaimed after church. "Pastor Mike kept talking about Adam and Eve in the Garden of Eden as though they were real people, but in my biology class at school, Ms. Kennedy said that human beings evolved over six million years in Africa. Which is it?"

"Well, it's a bit complicated," said Liz. "But, maybe both are true, in a sense, but in different ways."

There is actually a hidden question here. It is the question of the authority of the Bible for Christians. Some people argue that if the story of Adam and Eve is not historically accurate, then the historical accuracy of the accounts of Jesus's life, death, and resurrection, which are at the core of the Christian faith, should also be

Augustine of Hippo, 354-430

called into question. However, Christians have not always tied their claim of the authority of the Bible to its historical accuracy. The claim that the Bible must be historically accurate in every respect, sometimes called "biblical inerrancy," arose primarily among Protestant Christians in the eighteenth and nineteenth centuries.

An older and more common understanding of the authority of the Bible dates back at least as far as **Augustine** in the fifth century BCE. It holds that the Bible is infallible or unfailing in matters it teaches regarding Christian theological belief and practice but accepts that the text was written to accommodate the understanding of the world held by its readers and hearers. Augustine adopted this "principle of accommodation" when interpreting scripture.

So, the Bible could include understandings of nature, say the view that the Sun travels around the Earth, because that was the understanding of nature of the biblical writers at the times in which books of the Bible were written.

As an example, Joshua is said to have stopped the movement of the Sun so

Martin Luther, 1483-1546

that it was "midday" for a whole day (Joshua 10.12–14). This reflects the common sense understanding that the Sun moves around the Earth. Even the Protestant reformers Martin Luther and John Calvin accepted an Earth-centered universe and objected to the Copernican Sun-centered model. But their objections were not theological or because they held that the Bible was absolutely accurate on every matter about which it spoke. Rather they observed that the idea that the

Earth travels around the Sun was contrary to ordinary day-to-day experience of nature. They thought Copernicus's system was foolish.

Today, because of later scientific discoveries, we know that such an Earth-centered understanding is mistaken. But astronomical discoveries in no way invalidate the theological authority of the Bible for Christians. Instead, such discoveries can enrich a Christian's appreciation of God's creation.

But specifically, what about the matter of Adam and Eve? Were they actual historical people? Does an evolutionary account of human origins require that the answer to that question be, "No"?

John Calvin, 1506-1564

Adam and Eve in the Garden of Eden
Peter Paul Reubens

First, it is important to recognize that there are two stories of the creation of human beings in the Bible, composed at different times and serving different purposes. The first story is found in Genesis 1:1–2:3, and according to contemporary biblical scholars, was composed in the sixth century BCE, perhaps shortly after the Babylonian exile of the people of Judah. This account includes the creation of the whole universe. It begins with the creation of light (order out of chaos) and ends with the creation of human beings, men and women together, as the last creatures to be created. Humans are distinguished from all other creatures in that the authors identify them as being created in the "image" and "likeness" of God. Humans are to be "fruitful and multiply," filling the Earth. They are to "master" the Earth and "have dominion" or rule over all other living things.

Creation of Eve by Michelangelo

The second creation story (Genesis 2:4–24) comes from an earlier time before the Babylonian exile. It focuses on the creation of humans. In this account, the man, Adam, is created first. The name, "Adam," is a play on Hebrew words, for he is created from the "adamah," the ground or dust. A garden is created for him and he is placed in it to "till and keep" it. Adam has work to do. Next, because it is not good that the man is alone, the beasts of the field and birds are created as companions for Adam and he gives each of these new creatures its name. But none is a fitting partner. So, the first woman is created from a rib taken from Adam. She is not an alien creature but is "flesh of his flesh."

While the first creation story places humanity in a cosmic context and emphasizes human fertility and power in the Earth's network of life, the second creation story emphasizes the unity of men and women as companions in life. But this second creation story also offers a more subtle expression of human authority in nature. This is reflected in Adam's naming of the animals. In the Hebrew cultural context a name is not simply a label. It contributes to the very being of a thing. Adam's naming of the animals is in a sense a completion of their creation.

This act of naming has continued to be an expression of human power in nature. In the biblical story, it is likely an allusion to the rise of agriculture when many plants and animals

Adam naming the animals. Mural by Barbara Jones, 1950s

were transformed from a wild to a domesticated state. In this process, humanity gave them names. This process of naming continues today, most commonly in our naming of pets but also in the way we name plants and animals, even wild ones, so that we can place them into an ordered system of life.

Aristotle, in the fourth century BCE, was one of the first humans to try to develop a system of classification t o give order to the many and diverse forms of life. His "ladder of nature" with plants at the bottom and humans at the top was adopted by later Christians and adapted into a hierarchy of creation.

Aristotle, 384-322 BCE

Carolus Linnaeus, in the eighteenth century CE, developed a system of classification to organize the roughly ten thousand species known in his day. It was said that "God created, Linnaeus organized." He put into consistent practice the use of two names to classify an organism: its genus and species. So, human beings are identified by their genus classification, *Homo*, and their species classification, *sapiens*. Linnaeus and others before him assumed

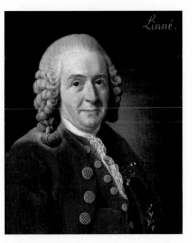

Carolus Linneaus, 1707-1778

Charles Darwin, 1809-182

that species were fixed, always the same from generation to generation. Linnaeus believed that variations in a species were deviations from an ideal type.

By the nineteenth century, there was an emerging recognition that species were not fixed but changed over time. When Charles Darwin published *On the Origin of Species by Means of Natural Selection, or the Preservation of Favoured Races in the Struggle for Life* in 1859, he provided the first comprehensive and systematic account of the process of the origin of species. In the first quarter of the twentieth century, Darwinian evolutionary theory was wedded to the science of genetics to produce the modern theory of evolution.

But what is a species? There is no simple answer to this simple question. There are many reasons why this is so. For example, there is the vast variation among living creatures. No two organisms are exactly the same. Even identical twins, as they grow, develop differences due to different life experiences. Nevertheless, there are a variety of ways that species are identified.

Perhaps the most common is the **"biological species concept"** as it was developed by Ernst Mayr in the last half of the twentieth century. According to this definition, a species is a population of organisms that can reproduce with one another but are reproductively isolated from other organisms. Unfortunately, this definition of species does not help with organisms like bacteria and some plants that do not reproduce sexually. Therefore, some scientists have suggested genetic criteria for discriminating between bacterial species.

Ernst Mayr 1904-2005

Although the precise definition of a species is somewhat ambiguous, there is broad consensus among scientists about the processes that have led to the vast variation of life forms on Earth. Given particular environmental conditions, some genes result in greater fertility or reproductive advantage. Organisms with such genes appear in greater numbers in the population. This is the process known as **natural selection**. Sometimes a natural event like a flood or earthquake can divide a population. The genetic differences between the separated groups can result in different evolutionary paths. The results are known as **genetic drift**.

The overall result is a branching process of speciation that forms what some call the "tree of life"—and might better be called the "bush of

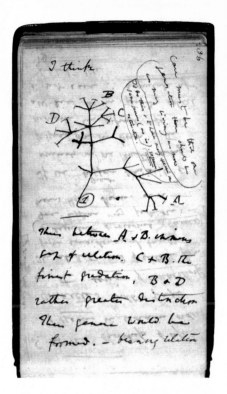

The "Tree of Life" from Darwin's notes

life" because it is not as tall as it is broad. Sometimes, evolution is depicted as a "parade" of species, for example from amphibians to *Homo sapiens*. But this image is misleading because it masks the branching process of what Darwin called "descent with modification."

Cluster 1	Cluster 2	Cluster 3
Ardipithicus Group	Australopithicus Group	Paranthropus Group
7.0-4.4 mya	4.2-2.0 mya	2.7-1.2 mya

Salhelanthropus tchadenis	Australopithicus afarensis	Paranthropus boisei
7-6 mya	3.85-2.95 mya	2.3-1.2 mya

Cluster 4
Home Group
1.8 mya-present

Homo erectus
1.8 mya-143 kya

Homo Heielbergensis
700-200 kya

Homo neanderthalensis
400-40 kya

Homo floresiensis
100-50 kya

The story of human evolution is one of branching that stretches back more than six million years since the separation of human and chimpanzee branches. Thus far at least nineteen species have been identified within this story. Together, these species are known as **hominins**, and all of them show evidence of upright posture and small canine, or "eye" teeth, in both males and females. These are traits found in humans today. These species do not form a single line of development but can be identified in successive historical clusters in which several species inhabited the Earth at the same time. These species can be organized as four clusters.

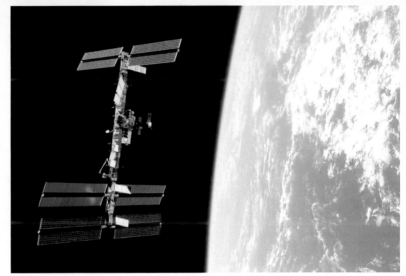

There is chronological overlap among the last three clusters. At various times there was more than one of these hominin species living on Earth. For the most part, they appear to have been reproductively isolated, though there is evidence that there may have been occasional interbreeding of **Homo neanderthalensis** and **Homo sapiens**. However, there is only one of these species that survives on Earth today, our species, **Homo sapiens.**

Today **Homo sapiens** is a world-shaping species.

There is virtually no place on the surface of the Earth where people have not made their home, often displacing other species. Where the land was not hospitable to human habitation, we have created artificial habitats (e.g., igloos in the Arctic and tents in the desert).

We have even extended the human habitat beyond the surface of Earth (e.g., living on the Moon briefly and extended living on the International Space Station).

Where we have found the natural surroundings insufficiently supportive we have technologically transformed them to accommodate our needs.

But what has any of this to do with Adam and Eve? Does this evolutionary account of human origins call into question their existence as actual historical persons? If so, is there any possibility that the two stories, the biblical story and the scientific story, can be understood as compatible?

Whether there can be a convergence of the stories rests in matters of judgment rather than in proof. There is no evidence in nature that all contemporary human beings descended from a single couple. However, there is ample evidence that all humans living today are one species, one human family. We humans are all one another's closest relatives in the evolutionary "family tree" of life.

There have been times in human history when one group of people has denied the humanity of some other group. There have been social, cultural, or political systems that divided people into separate "races" and held that only some "races" have genuine human status. There even have been Christians that held that some "races" were not descendants of Adam and so they were not human. But, there is no scientific biological support for such claims. On the contrary, the evolutionary history of life on Earth shows that all people living today comprise a single "human race"—evolutionary biology thus gives support to the metaphorical affirmation that all humans are "brothers and sisters." In fact, technically, we are all one another's "cousins."

What the biblical accounts of the creation definitely present are distinctive features of human nature: human proliferation on Earth; human power, especially in relation to other creatures, both plants and animals; the power of language (God speaks the creation into existence); and the participation of both humans (Gen. 2:18–19) and nonhuman creatures (Gen. 1:11–12, 20, 24) in the process of creation.

The scientific account of human origins encourages renewed appreciation of parts of the biblical account by pointing to elements of that story that might otherwise be missed. One example is the intimate interconnectedness of all life on Earth, including humans with other species. Another is the social character of human existence. Many species are social (e.g., ants and wolves) but *Homo sapiens* are powerfully so. Because the evolutionary process is one that occurs within populations, the very process is in a basic sense "social."

Interpersonal relationships provide community resources for adapting to the environment. It is interesting that in the Bible the differences between the male and female is not for the sake of procreation but in order to fulfill the need for sociality. Eve is created, according to the Bible, so that Adam will not be "alone" (Gen. 2:18–24).

The authors of the Bible recognized even in those ancient days what has become even more profoundly the case today. *Homo sapiens* are the dominant species on Earth. So, while the scientific story of the origin of humans and the biblical story of the creation of humans are not the same story, there is no essential conflict between them when each is appropriately understood. As Genesis in the second creation story depicts all land creatures and creatures of the air being made from the dust of the Earth, so evolutionary biology even more comprehensively has shown that *Homo sapiens* shares with **all** other species the same constituting material, DNA.

"But how can both be true?" pressed Will.

"Well, it's because the Bible isn't a science text. But, also, the sciences do not provide the ultimate framework for understanding who we are in the grand scheme of things," answered Liz. "The writers of the Bible told their story using the common understandings of nature in their day. What else could they use? At the same time, their intuitions about how to answer the question, 'What does it mean to be human,' are still in many ways as true today as they were thousands of years ago. And the sciences help us appreciate those insights in a more detailed and deep way.

"You know, even if there weren't two actual people named Adam and Eve, who were the originating parents of all human beings, as the Bible tells the story, the sciences of human origins have shown us that all human beings do have in fact, a family relationship with one another and that we need one another."

Discussion Questions

1   Some Christians hold that the Bible is "inerrant," others that it is "infallible." How would you distinguish between these terms?

2   Given the two stories in Genesis about the origin of the universe and human beings, what do you see that distinguishes them? Are they in some ways contradictory? How do you understand the differences?

3   What does the scientific metaphor of the "tree" or "bush" of life suggest about humanity's place in the history of nature?

4   The sciences describe an unbroken but transforming chain of parents and children reaching from the very first one-celled organisms on Earth to each of us individually. In relation to this natural history of the diversification of life, what role does the biblical stories of Adam and Eve play for Christians?

5   If your teenager asked you if Adam and Eve were real people, how would you respond?

III

What Does God Look Like?

"Mommy, what does God look like?" asked Diana one morning at breakfast.

"That's a good question, sweetie," her mother, Elizabeth, replied. "Why do you ask?"

"Well, in Sunday school yesterday, Ms. Phelps said we were all made in the image of God but she didn't say what God looks like."

"Hmm."

Perhaps the most mysterious passages in the Bible are those (Gen. 1:26–27) that declare that humans are "made in the image and likeness of God." In the first place this declaration is mysterious because no place in the rest of the Bible (the Hebrew scriptures or the New Testament) is the meaning of "image

God, Michelangelo,
Sistine Chapel, 1511

and likeness of God" specified. The mystery deepens when we take into account the Hebrew abhorrence of idolatry. Still, some Christian artists have depicted God. For example, Michelangelo shows God as an elderly but physically robust man with a flowing beard dwelling among the clouds surrounded by angelic creatures.

The Bible does use many anthropomorphic images to characterize God (e.g., shepherd, warrior, judge, father), but the Jewish, Christian, and Islamic traditions have always understood that these verbal images are metaphors, just as the artists' images are. However, if taken literally or absolutely, these images, verbal or artistic, become idols. The Ten Commandments explicitly prohibits making idols. So, to what does the expression, "image and likeness of God," refer?

Early Christian theologians were deeply influenced by classical Greek philosophers, most especially by Plato and his student, Aristotle. By the thirteenth century, Aristotle's philosophy had become the dominant intellectual framework within which to express Christian theology, most notably Thomas Aquinas's theology. Aquinas identified the ability to reason with "the image or likeness of God.

Some scientists study the similarities and differences among living creatures. Ethology is the study of how animals behave, particularly in their natural habitats. What does such study tell us about the uniqueness of human qualities? This science has shown that many behaviors that were once thought to be exclusively human can be found in other members of the animal kingdom. Behavior

Thomas Aquinas, 1225-1274

that we call cooperative, altruistic, and intelligent in humans can be observed in other species. A pod of killer whales will organize themselves to jointly create a wave that sweeps the seal from an ice flow. Such cooperative activity is not limited to hunting. Dolphins, killer whale near

cousins, have been observed supporting an ill or injured member of their group for many hours and bringing them to the surface of the water to breathe. In laboratory experiments, rats have been observed freeing a fellow rat from captivity even when there is no gain or reward for them as a result of the act.

In the twentieth century, some Jewish and Christian theologians like Martin Buber and Karl Barth associated the "image of God" with humans' capacity to have **distinctive relationships**, for example, **living in community** with other humans and especially with God. In particular, it is said that humans had the unique capacity to love as God loves.

Still others have seen the "image" as the human capacity to **"have dominion"** over nature. In 1967, historian **Lynn White** proposed that this latter understanding of "image" has led to human technological exploitation of nature in western culture.

The case also has been made that there is no single or unique human traits that distinguish *Homo sapiens* from other animals as possessors of "the image and likeness of God." Instead, the "image" is

Lynn Townsend White, 1907-1987

Mary Leakey at the site where she discovered the Australopithecus afarensis footprints at Laetoli, Tanzania, in 1976.

said to be a theological one granted to humans by virtue of God's initiative: **humans are elected** to be the image of God.

Although within western religious communities the meaning of the "image of God" remains ambiguous, paleoanthropologists, scientists that study the evidence related to human origins, have identified features that have come together to distinguish *Homo sapiens* as a species and determined roughly when these features appeared in the history of life.

The first feature is the **ability to walk on two feet.** Evidence has been found that some of our earliest relatives in the human family began walking upright as long as 6 MYA (million years ago). By 4 MYA, some of the descendants of these early humans were walking mostly on two feet. Seventy footprints of an early human relative, *Australopithecus afarensis*, were preserved in wet volcanic ash. These have been dated to 3.6 MYA.

While there are other species like chimpanzees that fashion simple tools (for example, using long grasses or thin twigs to "fish" for termites and even stones to open nuts), a human stone tool culture began to appear about 2.6 MYA and became more and more refined over time. These stone tools were purposefully made, not just useful pieces of natural rock picked up off the ground. A hammerstone was used to knock off a stone flake from a core stone. The result was not only a sharp-edged flake but also a sharp-edged core. By 1.6 MYA, stone hand axes and other larger stone tools were being produced.

Spears, with stone points attached to staffs, appeared by 100,000 years ago. At about this time, tools for preparing (scrapers) and perforating (awls) animal hides were being used. Toolmakers also began to employ a greater variety of materials, including bone, ivory and antlers.

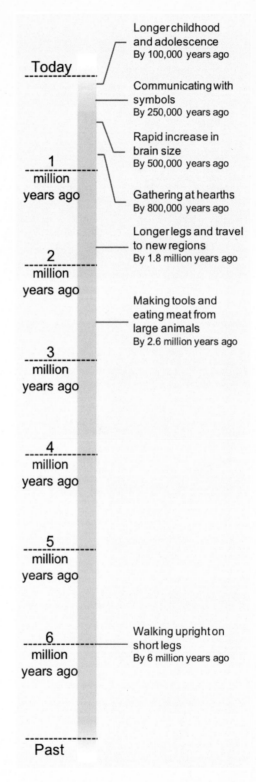

Today

Longer childhood and adolescence
By 100,000 years ago

Communicating with symbols
By 250,000 years ago

Rapid increase in brain size
By 500,000 years ago

1 million years ago

Gathering at hearths
By 800,000 years ago

Longer legs and travel to new regions
By 1.8 million years ago

2 million years ago

Making tools and eating meat from large animals
By 2.6 million years ago

3 million years ago

4 million years ago

5 million years ago

6 million years ago

Walking upright on short legs
By 6 million years ago

Past

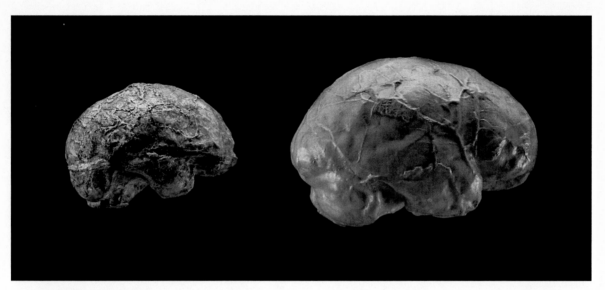

Endocasts of Homo erectus (left) and Homo sapiens (right) illustrate rapid growth in brain size

Even earlier, tool-making humans had discovered how to make and use fire. The earliest hearths are dated to about 790,000 years ago and evidence for the control of fire to cook food is at least that old. Fire not only changed human nutrition, it also provided a focal point for community life and a means of protection against predators.

The six million years of human evolution corresponds to a period of increased climate fluctuation. A rapid increase in human brain size corresponds to a period when climate change was greatest in frequency, extent, and severity. The need to adapt to climate-related environmental conditions seems to have been a selective factor for increased brain size and cognitive capacities.

The earliest human ancestors 6 MYA had brains only slightly larger than those of today's great apes, about the size of an orange. During the first four million years, brain size increased slowly to that of a grapefruit or about 800 cubic centimeters. Over the next two million years, brain size increased more rapidly to more than 1,700 cubic centimeters, the size of a cantaloupe. This is the brain size of *Homo neanderthalensis* and early *Homo sapiens* as long as 100,000 years ago. Gradual but accelerating increases of brain size correlate to both the increasing variability of Earth's climate and evidence for the development of more complex behaviors in the form of tool making and social and cultural life.

Homo neanderthalensis was an accomplished toolmaker and exhibited complex social behaviors, including caring for disabled members of the group and burying the dead. But it is among *Homo sapiens* that we first find evidence of the flowering of imagination, the complex process of representing the world in symbols and thinking about things not actually experienced in the world.

It is not possible to pinpoint when language, which is perhaps the most remarkable human capacity, first appeared in human history. Both *Homo neanderthalensis* and *Homo sapiens* possess a gene that regulates areas of brain development associated with language. This suggests that their common ancestor, *Homo heidelbergensis*, also possessed this gene, meaning that language capacity could reach back more than 200,000 years. While many animals communicate with vocalizations, and even nonhuman primates (for example, baboons, and gorillas) can be taught to communicate symbolically, none of these other species communicate in this manner in the wild. It is language and symbolic representation that lie at the foundation of distinctively human culture, including religion and science.

All of these features taken together make up the human "image": walking on two legs, tool use and innovation, control and use of fire, large brain-to-body ratio, and symbolic language. These features emerged slowly over 6 million years of natural history. Yet none of these features individually seems to correspond to what the biblical writers were seeking to express with the phrase "image of God."

It is probably true that the authors of Genesis 1 meant to identify the "image of God" with human beings alone, but the text as such does not require such an exclusive interpretation because "the image of God" is not explicitly denied for other creatures. In the opening of his Gospel, John sets the stage by identifying the primordial divine "Word" with a human person, Jesus of Nazareth. Jesus for Christians is the enfleshment or embodiment of that divine creative "Word."

John declares that this same "Word" also is involved intimately in the creation of everything that exists: "All things came into being through [the Word], and without him not one thing came into being." (John 1:1–3b) Perhaps a way of thinking about the "Word" is to identify it with God's intent or purpose.

In the end, we might answer the question about what it means to be made in the "image and likeness of God" by saying that it is about embodying God's purposes in the exercise of all those evolved features and capacities that have come to comprise human beings. But *all* creatures to some extent also embody God's intent. If the "image" is making divine intent concrete, then every creature, to the degree that they do so, would also be "made in the image and likeness of God."

Homo sapiens is arguably the most complex species on Earth. But that complexity is the consequence of the inheritance we have received from ancestral forms of life beginning with single living cells. There is a sense that we both inherit the "image of God" from all of those forms of life in our evolutionary biological lineage, and constitute that "image" anew as we respond faithfully to the call to enflesh the "Word" in our individual lives.

"You remember, Diana, when your art teacher at school said that you really put yourself into your art?" Elizabeth began.

"I do, Mommy," Diana replied. "She said she could tell it was me who drew the picture just by looking at it."

"But the picture wasn't a picture of you was it?"

"No," answered Diana.

Elizabeth continued, "Well, you might think of 'the image of God' as something like that: God expressing God's self in each part of creation like you expressed yourself in your painting."

"So, I'm a picture of God?" asked Diana enthusiastically.

"Sort of, but not exactly. Imagine if, when you were painting your picture, the paintbrush and the paper and the paints themselves were alive and could do anything they wanted. What kind of picture would you get then?" Elizabeth asked.

Diana scrunched up her face and said emphatically, "That could be a mess."

"So," Elizabeth went on, "for it to be the picture you wanted, for it to be an expression of you, the brush and paper and paint would have to behave as you intended them to behave. You remember when we were in the restaurant last week and that nice lady at the next table said how good a reflection you were of me as a mommy? It was because you were behaving like I wanted you to. You might think of being made in the 'image of God' as you behaving in a way that expresses God's intention for you."

"Hmm," mused Diana as she headed off to her room to finish getting ready for school.

Discussion Questions

1 Christians have used many human images to describe God. What images are particularly important to you?

2 When you read the opening verses of the Gospel of John, what do you think he meant when he wrote, "All things came into being through [the Word], and without him not one thing came into being"? (John 1:1–3b)

3 Over centuries, Christians have identified many human characteristics individually or as a group as signifying what the Bible means by the phrase "image and likeness of God." What do you think the phrase refers to?

4 In what ways do discoveries in the sciences of human evolution contribute to an understanding of the meaning of the phrase made in the "image and likeness of God?"

5 What significance does the meaning of the phrase have with respect to human beings' relationships to the rest of creation?

6 If an eight-year-old asked you what God looked like, how would you respond?

IV

Accident or Plan?

"Hey, Dad, am I an accident?" Will asked his father.

"No, Will!" Jack answered a bit too quickly. "Your mom and I planned for both you and your sister. In fact…"

"No, no. That's not what I meant. We were talking about evolution in school and the teacher said that it's based on random variation. After class, my friend Teddy said that that was all wrong, that his pastor said the universe was designed by God and we are all part of God's plan."

One of the objections that some Christians have to an evolutionary explanation of the history of the universe is that evolution seems to suggest that the way things have come about is by happenstance, by accident. But does an evolutionary understanding require this conclusion? In particular, are human beings simply a cosmic accident or was the universe designed so that human beings would be a part of it? These are not simple yes or no questions.

One thing that makes the theory of biological evolution so powerful is its simplicity. There are two basic elements that account for the history and diversity of life on Earth: **genetic variation** and **natural selection**.

However, the processes that bring about variation have no apparent goal. The variation may be helpful to the organism or it may be lethal. The processes of variation are simply stimulants for change whether for good or for ill.

So, from the point of view of variation there is no direction involved. Genetic variation, apart from deliberate human intervention, is the result of happenstance. But this fact doesn't mean we can conclude the evolutionary process as a whole is without direction.

First, variations do not occur in a vacuum. They occur within some environmental context. In relation to that environment, the variation can be advantageous, disadvantageous, or neutral. You only have to consider the variety of wildflowers on Earth today to appreciate the power of the environment working on variation to create diversity. The effect of the environment to determine that some variations are advantageous and others disadvantageous is what is known as **natural selection**. Genetic variations that adapt well to their environment are perpetuated into future generations. Those variations that do not adapt well are less likely to be found the future. So, environmental adaptation sets an initial standard for "direction." For this reason, it is incorrect to say that evolution is only a random process; it is a process in which the environment determines what genetic variations will survive, flourish, and produce offspring.

Sometimes different environmental contexts have similar adaptive challenges. This can result in what is known as **"convergent evolution."** For example, the structure of the "camera eye" evolved separately in squid, jellyfish, and mammals. This convergence is a kind of direction. But, again, it is direction evoked by environmental conditions, not by apparent purposeful intervention.

At the same time, the environment itself is always only relatively stable. In fact, environmental instability has been a significant factor in the development of early humans' brains, where the intellectual capacity to respond to rapidly and substantially changing environmental conditions were adaptive.

When it comes to *Homo sapiens*, there are those, including some scientists like Freeman Dyson, who have concluded that the possibility of human existence is so dependent on particular basic features of the universe that the existence of human beings was built in from the beginning. This idea is referred to as the **"Cosmological Anthropic Principle."** In this strong form it suggests that the original conditions of the universe, its basic parameters and the constants of nature, were "fine tuned" such that human life **WOULD** evolve. This is a deterministic understanding of the processes of nature that led to *Homo sapiens*. It implies the working out in natural history of a preexisting purpose.

Freeman Dyson, Physicist,
1923-present

"In some sense the universe
knew we were coming."

Brandon Carter,
1942-present

Physicist who in 1973 proposed
the original "anthropic principle"

However, originally the "Anthropic Principle" made a more limited claim. In this weak form it simply asserted that whatever the basic parameters of the universe are, whatever the universe's most basic constants and laws, they must be such that *Homo sapiens* **CAN** occur. We are here, after all. Stated this way, the "anthropic principle" is a tool that can help identify what those constants and laws are, but it does not mean that *Homo sapiens* are a necessary outcome of the history of nature. This understanding of the "Anthropic Principle" reflects a probabilistic view of the processes of nature.

For the Christian, is the deterministic understanding of the "Anthropic Principle" to be preferred over the probabilistic one? There are some Christians who hold that God created each type or kind of organism individually. This makes each type of creature, especially human beings, the direct result of divine intent and so no accident. This is a very deterministic view. Other Christians hold that God set the initial conditions of the created order in such a way that the process of nature led inevitably to the development of *Homo sapiens.* These Christians do not see God intervening here and there to create this or that thing but rather creating a natural system with the outcome that God desires built in from the beginning. Again, this is a relatively deterministic view.

A third Christian view holds that God is actively calling the creation to create itself, as suggested in the first chapter of Genesis (Genesis 1:11, 20, 24). In this view, God's purpose is not to create this or that particular thing but rather to create a rich and beautiful whole. Richness is created through variety and complexity, while beauty emerges from the way in which that complex variety fits together as a whole. This is a more probabilistic view. No particular thing is a necessary outcome of the process of creation. Many things could comprise different whole creations that each is richly beautiful in the coherence of its complex diversity. For example, a brilliant blue wall may be beautiful, but it is not a rich beauty. A wall made of many differently colored pebbles may exhibit a rich chaos of color, but each of the bits of color may so clash with the others that the wall's wholeness, and so its beauty, is undermined. A mosaic wall (a creation of many and diverse creatures) in which all the bits of color are united with one another as contrasts (a cosmic ecosystem uniting stars to quarks and bacteria to *Homo sapiens*) creates a rich complexity of beauty. With this third view, you could say that the universe (and so every constituent, including *Homo sapiens*) is purposeful but that no particular thing in the creation is necessary.

So, to the question, "Are *Homo sapiens*, human beings, the result of happenstance or an expression of a divine plan?" a possible answer is, "Yes."

"Well, Will," Jack answered after a moment. "It may be hard to understand but it could be both. I mean, the outcome of God's creation could be both determined and undetermined. For instance, take a coin flip. You know ahead of time that it is going to be either heads or tails, that's fixed. But until you actually flip the coin you don't know which it will be, unless you're using that loaded coin your friend, Teddy, gave you."

"OK, I get that," Will replied. "But does that mean life is a loaded coin toss? If God is Creator, doesn't that mean the result of the coin toss is already decided?"

Jack thought for a moment. "Let me try another analogy. When your football coach worked with your team before last week's game, he had y'all run the same plays over and over to get them just right, didn't he?"

"Sure," answered Will.

"But in the game, how many of those plays went exactly as designed? And there was even a touchdown on that broken play when your quarterback was chased out of the pocket. Football has rules that set the boundaries for the way the game is played. And teams put together plans for how they want the game to go. But, the actual game cannot be predicted ahead of time. In a technical philosophical sense, it's accidental."

"OK, I see that too," Will said. "But that doesn't explain how God gets the creation God wants if the outcome is so uncertain."

"To be honest," Jack admitted, "this is not a simple question and Christian thinkers much wiser than me have wrestled with it for centuries. Let me try one last analogy. Imagine that God wants the creation to produce something. But the thing to be produced is not a particular thing but a quality—for example, beauty. Like the options in a coin toss or the rules for football, a framework is set so that something definite, beauty (or a coin toss result or a football game) will be produced. But God does not determine how that will be done. The beauty could come in the form of a painting, a statue, a song or symphony, an inspiring essay, or even an uplifting comedy improv. There is uncertainty about or freedom to determine how the beauty will be produced but not whether it will be produced. This isn't a final answer to the question but maybe it's something to think about."

Will rubbed his forehead. "That's a lot to think about. Maybe we could ask Pastor Mike about it this next Sunday and see what he has to say."

Discussion Questions

1   What experiences do you have day to day that seem predetermined? Or experiences that seem random or accidental?

2   Do you find in your own life story a combination of predetermination and randomness? If so, what are some examples of each?

3   Read the following passages: Genesis 12:1–3, Exodus 1:8–2:10, Mark 14:32–42. In what ways do these stories seem predetermined? In what ways do they seem random or accidental? In what ways can they be seen as probabilistic?

4   If *Homo sapiens* are the result of an evolutionary process that is both deterministic (e.g., natural selection) and random (e.g., genetic variation), how do you understand human beings as God's creation?

5   If a teenager were to ask you if he or she was an accident or part of God's plan, how would you respond?

V

Why Did They Have to Die?

"Mommy, why did the dinosaurs have to die?" asked Diana as they left the science center's traveling dinosaur exhibit. "I thought God loved all his creatures. You know we sing that song in church about 'all things bright and beautiful, all things great and small, the good Lord made them all.' But if God made them and God is love, why did they all have to die?"

This may be one of humanity's most ancient questions. In its classic form it goes something like: if God is all good and God is all powerful, why is there evil in the world? Here "evil" does not refer to some villain but rather to the pain and suffering and, most especially, death that all living things experience. In Christian theology, this is the classical issue of **theodicy**. An evolutionary understanding of

Alfred Lord Tennyson, 1808-1892

the history of nature and of the origin of human beings seems to make this issue even worse. The history of life on Earth is a profound history of death.

Some Christians object to identifying God's creative activity with the process of evolution precisely because it involves so much loss of life. Even if Darwin's religious views were influenced by many factors in his personal history, he also found the carnage in the history of life to be religiously troubling. Alfred Lord Tennyson wrote of "nature, red in tooth and claw" nine years prior to Darwin publishing his *On the Origin of Species by Means of Natural Selection, or the Preservation of Favoured Races in the Struggle for Life* in 1859.

One type of relationship among the various species is that of predator and prey. But it seems that ultimately everything is eaten by everything else as organic material is recycled through natural history. But pain and death are more than simply a part of the struggle for life. Processes of extinction that result in the demise of whole species are an integral part of the evolutionary process. Extinctions open up habitats for new species. The extinctions of the great dinosaurs 65 million years ago (MYA) opened up habitats in which mammals could flourish and evolve. Looking back, the evolutionary path from such disasters

eventually led to the emergence of *Homo sapiens*, us.

It has been estimated that 99.9 percent of all species that have ever lived on planet Earth have become extinct. Given that there are today more than 1.7 million living species of animals, plants, and algae, the number of extinct species according to the estimate would be astronomical. So much loss of life, to say nothing of the suffering such loss represents. How can an evolutionary process that involves such calamity be the creative means of a beneficent deity?

Job and this friends

This is one way of identifying the general theological issue of theodicy. On a personal level, it is the religious issue that underlies the plaintive question in the face of innocent pain, suffering, and death: Why me? It is the biblical character Job's question to the heavens.

To be candid, no one in any religious tradition has ever been able to offer a completely satisfactory answer to this question. On the one hand, from a Christian theological perspective, no creature is necessary. No creature has to exist. This ensures the "mortality" of all things. One philosopher, Alfred North Whitehead, has described this formal vulnerability as "perpetual perishing." But for Christians there is a kind of logic to this vulnerability.

Perhaps the most fundamental thing a Christian can say about God is "God is love." But love cannot be coerced or forced. Love is a gift that can only be given out of freedom. Yet freedom is a two-edged sword. If it makes love possible, it also

Christ at the Cross, Carl Bloch, 1870

makes hate possible. If it makes it possible for one creature to care for another, it also makes it possible for one creature to exploit another. For Christians, the crucifixion is an iconic symbol for both human inhumanity and also of the depth of divine love. In the face of natural selection and extinctions, the whole creation can be seen as cruciform. The history of nature manifests the destruction freedom makes possible, but also the triumph of creativity over destruction, the victory of life over death.

So, it may have been inevitable that dinosaurs would die, but it wasn't necessary that dinosaurs died in a mass extinction. Still, as a consequence of their death, more creatures of wondrous sorts came into being, evolved.

"You know, kiddo, sometimes you ask the hardest questions," Liz responded to her daughter. "What you are asking about is one of the hardest questions anyone at church, even Pastor Mike, could ever try to answer."

"But I want to know. It seems mean for God to kill the dinosaurs," insisted Diana.

"First, it's not quite right to say that God 'killed the dinosaurs' any more than God killed your grandfather, who lived to be ninety-six, or that God killed Goldy, your goldfish, last year. Part of being one of God's creatures is that we have both a beginning and an end. We are born and we die. Actually, we do have some 'dinosaurs' still around. That cardinal, outside the window there, is a descendant of dinosaurs from long ago, just like you are a descendant of Grampa Joe.

"Another thing, God's love does not depend on how long a thing lives. As the song says, 'God loves all creatures, great and small.' It could also say 'long-lived and short-lived,' as well. There are some parts of God's creation that last much, much shorter than the blink of an eye, but God loves them as much as that tortoise we saw at the zoo that was more than one hundred years old."

"But, I guess what I don't understand, Mommy, is why **anything** has to suffer or die, if God loves them," persisted Diana.

"That's a really mysterious and hard question. Truthfully, I don't think anyone has the final answer to it. But maybe one way to think about it is like this. If I could control everything you did so that you would never make a mistake or hurt yourself, would you still be my lovely Diana, who sometimes skins her knee and asks the darnedest questions? You might be an indestructible robot like the ones Will battles in his video game, but you would not be you. You are full of surprises just like the rest of God's creation. And sometimes those surprises can hurt. But, because you are free to be surprising, you are also free to love. Love is a gift that we give. It isn't something that can be required or programmed in. The freedom that makes love possible is the same freedom that makes life risky. And I can tell from your expression that I'm not being real clear. But, that is part of the problem with your very good question. Any answer seems to be murky to start with."

Discussion Questions

1   In what ways do you find that life seems unfair? Where in nature does life seem unfair?

2   Extinctions, and death in general, seem to be essential parts of the evolutionary process. Does this seem to be an impediment to understanding God's creation in an evolutionary way?

3   How might God's response to Job (Job 38–41) apply to an understanding of evolution as God's way of creating?

4   How do you think the sciences and Christianity approach the deep mystery of creation? In similar or different ways?

5   How could the sciences and Christianity contribute to each other's approach to this mystery of creation?

6   If an eight year old were to ask you why God allows death and suffering in creation, how would you respond?

VI

Are We in Charge?

"Dad, are we really stewards of creation like Pastor Mike said?" asked Will as they drove away from church. "I know it's going to be Earth Day soon and all, but are we really responsible for all of creation? That seems like an awful lot to me. I mean, are we really in charge?"

The question of humanity's place in nature is one that is probably as old as the possibility of *Homo sapiens* sitting around a campfire at night with moments not committed to mere survival. The Bible actually offers several visions of how humans are related to the rest of creation, at least the creation that is the Earth and its biosphere.

In Genesis 1:28, humans are instructed to "Be fruitful and multiply, and fill

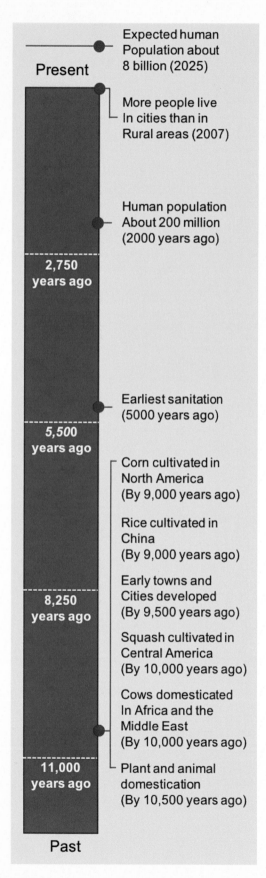

Present

Expected human
Population about
8 billion (2025)

More people live
In cities than in
Rural areas (2007)

Human population
About 200 million
(2000 years ago)

2,750
years ago

Earliest sanitation
(5000 years ago)

5,500
years ago

Corn cultivated in
North America
(By 9,000 years ago)

Rice cultivated in
China
(By 9,000 years ago)

8,250
years ago

Early towns and
Cities developed
(By 9,500 years ago)

Squash cultivated in
Central America
(By 10,000 years ago)

Cows domesticated
In Africa and the
Middle East
(By 10,000 years ago)

11,000
years ago

Plant and animal
domestication
(By 10,500 years ago)

Past

the earth and subdue it; and have dominion over the fish of the sea and over the birds of the air and over every living thing that moves upon the earth." These are martial and regal assignments. This passage suggests an image of delegated authority. The creation may ultimately belong to the Creator, but humankind has been given charge to rule over it on God's behalf. It has been argued that within the Abrahamic traditions (Judaism, Christianity, Islam) this passage has been taken as divine warrant to exploit nature.

Only a few verses later, in Genesis 2:15, it is written, "The Lord God took the man and put him in the Garden of Eden to till it and keep it." This evokes a diff erent image of humanity's relationship with the rest of the living world, one of stewardship and management. To be sure, humans are still in charge. But the task is not to "subdue" or "dominate" but to "till" and "keep." In recent history, this passage has been taken by Christians to encourage a more ecologically construc- tive relationship with other forms of life, the role of steward.

Still, within the second chapter of Genesis there is the intimation of one more sense of the relation of human beings to other living creatures, namely, that of kin. First, it is said, "then the Lord God formed man from the dust of the ground, and breathed into his nostrils the breath of life; and the man became a living being." (Genesis 2:7) The Hebrew word for "living being" is **nephesh**. A few verses further along when God is seeking to create a helpmate for Adam it is said that "So out of the ground the Lord God formed every animal of the field and every bird of the air, and brought them to the man to see what he would call them; and whatever the man called each living creature, that was its name." (Genesis 2:19) Here the phrase "living creature" is also the word **nephesh**. Not only are the human and the animals made of the same "dirt," but also they apparently share the same animating divine breath. In the story they appear to be "kin" by being made of the same stuff and by the same process.

This last passage also identifies a hierarchical relationship between humanity and other life: Adam gives the animals their names. We have already discussed this passage earlier, but the important feature here is the relative power the human exercises with respect to the animals even in the face of their creaturely kinship.

In one respect the scientific study of nature reinforces this last vision by linking all species in a network of biological kinship. Paleoanthropology also provides an account of how the evolution of **Homo sapiens** is a history of increasing power in the Earth's evolutionary ecosystem. Our hominin ancestors not only moved into new habitats (from forests to savannas) and persevered in climatically unstable habitats, but also with the mastery of stone tools and fire they began to transform habitats to make them more accommodating for human survival. As suggested earlier, the biblical "naming of the animals" is likely a reference both to increasing human knowledge of nature and the act of domesticating the plants and animals that were named.

The result has been habitat transformation on a global scale. **Homo sapiens** has become an often unintentional selective force in the evolution of life on Earth. Humans may not be "in charge," but we are certainly powerful and have had and continue to have profound impacts on the global ecology.

It is in regard to these relationships of power that Christians who understand humanity's "place in nature" to be ultimately a "gift of God" need to

remember another biblical declaration. The Gospel of Luke includes these words: "From everyone to whom much has been given, much will be required; and from one to whom much has been entrusted, even more will be demanded." (Luke 12:48)

So, are we "in charge?" The obvious answer is no, but there is a "but." The time that *Homo sapiens* have existed on Earth may be dwarfed by the age of the Earth (4.6 billion years) and of life (3.8 billion years), to say nothing of the age of the universe (13.8 billion years). Our place may be dwarfed by the scope of the universe (between 100 and 300 sextillion stars—one or three followed by twenty-three zeros). Nevertheless, on Earth for the past six million years, we, following our hominin ancestors, have become a formidable force in the global ecosystem. We are the five-hundred-pound gorilla in the room. Therefore, the consequences of human behavior, both deliberate and unintended, have great significance for all life on Earth. *Homo sapiens* may not have a divine mandate to rule, but by virtue of the power we possess as a species we inescapably have responsibility for the impact our living has on the rest of the biosphere.

"You're right, of course, Will," Jack admitted. "God's creation is pretty big. Like that NOVA episode we watched, we now know there are almost a countless number of galaxies. Even our own galaxy, the Milky Way, is huge, with billions upon billions of stars, to say nothing of planets. Every week, almost, we are confirming a newly discovered planet. So, it would be pretty silly to think we are 'in charge' of all of that. I don't actually think that was what Pastor Mike was saying."

"But even on Earth," Will pressed," how much control do we actually have?"

"Well, as hurricanes and tornadoes and tsunamis and earthquakes show every year we often have less control than we think we have," Jack acknowledged. "But, at the same time we have a lot of power, sometimes more power than we realize."

"What do you mean?" Will asked.

"Well, I doubt that when they first began building coal-fired factories in England at the beginning of the Industrial Revolution, or when Henry Ford began to produce the first consumer automobiles, anyone thought these would contribute to changing the very climate of our planet. Between the growth of the human population and the related expansion of the use of carbon-based technologies, humans are having a profound impact on the whole planet," Jack suggested.

"So, what Pastor Mike was getting at is that we have a responsibility to be good stewards of the resources of the Earth that we have access to?" offered Will.

"I think that is nearer what he meant," agreed Jack. "But you know, even though I agree that we should not waste natural resources, I wonder sometimes if the idea of being 'God's Steward' on Earth still gives us too much credit, that it suggests we have a superior managerial responsibility within the Earth's ecosystem. What the evolutionary sciences seem to show is that while we are a powerful species in that ecosystem, our relationship with our fellow creatures is not one of a superior nature but one of kinship. The Bible says that all Christians are 'brothers and sisters' in Christ, but it seems to me the sciences point out we are 'cousins' with all other living things on Earth. I wonder how we would treat the other living things around us differently, if we actually thought of them as our relatives? And how might that be related to Jesus's command to love our neighbor as ourselves?"

Discussion Questions

1   What consequence do you think the biblical mandate to "subdue and have dominion" over the other living creatures on Earth has had in human history?

2   What consequence do you think the biblical charge to "tend and keep" the garden has had in human history?

3   How does the biblical parable of the talents (Matthew 25:14–30) bear on the relation of *Homo sapiens* to the Earth and other species viewed as resources?

4   How might what we learn about the origin and development of *Homo sapiens* bear on our understanding of the role of humans in nature?

5   If a teenager asked you what responsibility we have toward our fellow creatures, how would you respond?

MORE OF THE STORY

Anthropic principle: In 1973, Brandon Carter proposed an "anthropic principle." His conclusion was that the basic features of the universe had to allow for the evolution of human beings because we are here. This is sometimes called the "weak" anthropic principle. Its use is that it limits the range in which the basic parameters of the universe must exist. Some scientists and theologians have gone beyond this position and articulated a "strong" anthropic principle; namely, that the basic parameters of the universe are especially "fine tuned" in order that humankind would appear in the course of natural history.

Thomas Aquinas (1225–1274): Thomas Aquinas, a thirteenth-century Roman Catholic theologian, is one of the chief examples of what is referred to as the "medieval synthesis"; that is, the synthesis of recently recovered classical philosophy, primarily that of Aristotle, with traditional Christian theology. During his day, however, this synthesis was so novel that it was suspected of being heretical. In 1277, three years after Thomas's death, twenty of his "propositions" were found on a list of 219 condemned by the Bishop of Paris. However, by the middle of the seventeenth century, in the midst of the Protestant Reformation during the Roman Catholic Counter-Reformation, the Council of Trent considered Thomas's theology to be the standard of Christian orthodoxy. The theology of Thomas Aquinas continues today to have substantial influence in the Roman Catholic Church.

Following Aristotle, Thomas identified three types of souls. The vegetative or nutritive soul is exhibited in plants that grow and develop by drawing sustenance from the earth and sun. Animals have nutritive features, but in addition, they move readily from place to place and respond to various sensory stimuli. So, Aquinas, borrowing from Aristotle, identified this feature of animals as their sensitive and animative soul. Humans not only grow and develop, they are not only sensitive to light and heat and move around, but also they decide things. They think. As Aristotle described human beings as the "rational animal" so Aquinas understood humans to possess a "rational soul."

Augustine of Hippo (354–430): Augustine was born in North Africa of a Christian mother and a father who did not convert to Christianity until his death-bed. He himself did not convert to the Christian faith until he was thirty-two. Still, he became one of the most influential theologians not only of his day but down through the ages in the Christian community. During his day, he addressed many questions concerning the meaning of the Christian faith and the non-Christian classical culture in which he lived. With regard to matters of science, religion, and the Bible, one of his most significant declarations is found in his book, *De Genesi ad litteram* (*The Literal Meaning of Genesis*).

"Often a non-Christian knows something about the earth, the heavens, and the other parts of the world, about the motions and orbits of the stars and even their sizes and distances…and this knowledge he holds with certainty from reason and experience. It is thus offensive and disgraceful for an unbeliever to hear a Christian talk nonsense about such things, claiming that what he is saying is based in Scripture. We should do all that we can to avoid such an embarrassing situation, which people see as ignorance in the Christian and laugh to scorn." (1:19:39)

Liger
(lion father/tiger mother)

Tiglon/Tigon
(tiger father/lion mother)

"Biological species concept": A species is a population of organisms that can reproduce with one another but are reproductively isolated from other organisms. In this definition, the term "isolation" is key. It can mean that if the organisms attempt to reproduce and actually do produce offspring, these offspring are infertile. For example, the mule, the result of mating a male donkey with a female horse, is infertile. But isolation can also mean that, by virtue of habitat and geographic distribution or behavior of the organisms in the wild, they do not reproduce even if they were otherwise capable. Crossbreeding lions and tigers, which are the same genus but different species, results in fertile offspring (ligers and tiglons/tigons) but such interspecies breeding does not occur in the wild.

Clusters in Human Evolution

The Ardipithicus Group (7.0–1.4 million years ago): The four species in this group (*Sahelanthropus tchadensis, Orrorin tugenensis, Ardipithicus kadabba, Ardipithicus ramidus)* are the first to exhibit significant bipedal behavior or walking on two legs. They also show a reduction in the size of their canine teeth. Brain size, however, was small, about the same size as in today's chimpanzees.

The Australopithecus Group (4.2–2.0 MYA): Species in this group (*Australopithecus anamensis, A. afarensis, A. garhi, A. afi canus, A. sediba*) show increased reliance on two-legged walking while retaining long arms and fingers adapted for tree climbing. These features gave them the flexibility of living in different habitats. Later species of this group are the first to use stone tools.

The Paranthropus Group (2.7–1.2 MYA): These species (*Paranthropus aethepicus, P. boisei, P. robustus)* show facial and jaw muscles especially adapted to a diet of tough foods. Members of this group lived alongside both earlier *Australopithecus* and later hominin species.

The Homo Group (1.8 MYA–present): These species show the control of fire, the development of more sophisticated tools and other forms of material culture. A recent fossil discovery indicates that there was another *Homo* species that shared an origin with Neanderthals. These are the Denisovans, whose fossil was found in the Altai Mountains of Siberia in 2008. The individual fossil dates from 41 KYA thousand yeas ago. Our own species, *Homo sapiens*, reaches back 200,000 years. We are the last remaining species in our group. In addition to the members of the genus *Homo* shown in the text there are *H. habilis, H. rudolfensis, H. naledi, H. Denisova*).

Hominin fossils continue to be discovered.

Convergent evolution: Sometimes two species that are very distant in the family "tree of life" nevertheless develop very similar features (e.g., the eyes of squids and humans). The similarity is not due to direct inheritance between the two species. Instead, it is due to similar responses in each family line to similar environmental selective factors. Because they face similar environmental challenges, their evolution converges toward similar features.

Nicolaus Copernicus (1473–1543): In the early sixteenth century, Nicolaus Copernicus, mathematician, Roman Catholic Church administer, and advisor to the King of Poland on monetary policy, was troubled by certain problems with the prevailing Earth-centered model of the universe. This model was based on Aristotle's natural philosophy of the fourth century BCE and had been geometrically expressed by Claudius Ptolemy in the second century CE. Copernicus discovered that Sun-centered astronomical models first proposed by the Pythagoreans in the third century BCE resolved these problems. He circulated a summary of his Pythagorean-inspired Sun-centered model, but largely set the work aside to pursue other matters. It was a young Lutheran mathematician, Georg Rheticus, who persuaded Compernicus to prepare a full mathematical treatment of his model for publication. Rheticus was not able to see the project through but enlisted another Lutheran, Andreas Ossiander, to see that the work was published. Copernicus received a copy of the publication, *De revolutionibus orbium coelestium* (*On the Revolutions of the Celestial Orbs*), shortly before his death.

Like many of his Christian intellectual contemporaries at the dawn of modern science, Copernicus's motivation for the study of nature was deeply religious. It is reported that he wrote:

"To know the mighty works of God, comprehend His wisdom and majesty and power, to appreciate in degree the wonderful working of His laws, surely all this must be a pleasing and acceptable mode of worship to the Most High to whom ignorance can not be more grateful than knowledge." From Poland: The Knight Among Nations (1907) by Louis E. Van Norman, p. 290.

Pierre Teilhard de Chardin, SJ (1881–1955): Fr. Pierre Teilhard de Chardin, SJ, was a French Jesuit paleontologist who was part of the French research team that discovered "Peking man." Teilhard sought a way to integrate scientific discoveries about nature, particularly natural history, the history of life, and the evolution of humankind with traditional Roman Catholic theology. However, the results of his efforts were sufficiently novel that beginning in 1925, some in the hierarchy of the Roman Catholic Church, as well as his Jesuit order, not only required that he neither teach nor publish his views, they also ordered that his works not be retained by libraries of Roman Catholic institutions. Much of his innovative theological writing was not published until after his death in 1955.

Perhaps one of the most concise statements of the challenge that faces Christians who accept an interactive view of the relationship of science and the Christian faith appears in a personal letter Teilhard wrote in 1947:

"When we speak of a 'theology of modern science,' it obviously does not mean that by itself science can determine an image of God and a religion. But what it does mean, if I am not mistaken, is that, given a certain development of science, certain representations of God and certain forms of worship are ruled out, as ***not being homogeneous*** with the dimensions of the universe known to our experience. This notion of homogeneity is without doubt of central importance in intellectual, moral and mystical life. Even though the various stages of our interior life cannot be expressed strictly in terms of one another, on the other hand they must agree in scale, in nature and tonality. Otherwise it would be impossible to develop a true spiritual unity in ourselves—and that is perhaps the most legitimate, the most imperative and most definitive of the demands made by man of today and man of tomorrow." From a personal letter written in 1947 and published in ***Science and Christ*** (Harper & Row, 1965).

Rene Descartes (1596–1650): The French philosopher, Descartes, was influenced by the Galileo controversy. He had placed a manuscript, ***La Monde***, with a publisher in the Netherlands when he heard of Galileo's condemnation. In that manuscript, Descartes had adopted a Copernican or Sun-centered model of the universe. However, because of his commitment to Roman Catholicism, he withdrew it from the publisher. *La Monde* was only published in its entirety after his death.

Descartes sought to make a space for both a basic revisioning of previous understandings of nature and the continuation of traditional Christian, particularly Roman Catholic, theology by separating science from religion. He divided the universe into diff erent substances: material and spiritual. He divided knowledge into two domains: acquired and revealed. He divided the human person: body and mind/spirit.

Galileo Galilei (1564–1642): Galileo helped establish the foundational principles of "modern science" and the "scientifi c method." As both an observer of nature and an experimentalist, he not only was the fi rst to report on the use of the telescope to observe heretofore unknown features of the planets (e.g., the craters on the moon, the phases of Venus, the moons of Jupiter), he also demonstrated that the acceleration of gravity is constant regardless of the mass of the object falling.

His observations and experiments convinced him that the generally accepted science derived form classical Greek scholars (predominately Aristotle) was mistaken and was particularly drawn to the Sun-centered cosmology of Copernicus.

However, he was instructed by authorities—by the Pope himself in the Roman Catholic Church—that he was not to promote this view because there was no observational or rational demonstration of heliocentrism, and the Bible clearly assumed an Earth-centered cosmology. The Pope did allow Galileo to write about both sides of the issue so long as he did not promote one side over the other.

In 1632, Galileo published *Dialogue Concerning the Two Chief World Systems* in which he not only clearly advocated Copernicus's view that the Earth revolved around the Sun and rotated on its own axis, but he placed some of the Pope's words to the contrary in the mouth of the character, Simplicio, who, as his name suggests, was something of a simpleton.

Galileo was called before the Roman Inquisition and required to recant his Copernican views. He was sentenced to house arrest in his villa in Arcetri, Italy, just outside of Florence. Ironically, it was there that he wrote perhaps his most important scientific work, *Discourses and Mathematical Demonstrations Relating to Two New Sciences,* which was published in 1638.

Genetic drift: A natural event like a landslide or the change in the path of a riverbed can divide a population. In such cases, the two now separated populations will not have the same gene frequencies and so their reproductive futures will take different paths. If this separation results in long-term reproductive isolation, a new species can be formed.

Genetic variation: Offspring vary from their parents and from one another. When Charles Darwin first proposed his theory for the origin of species in 1859, he could observe such variations both in the wild and among the pigeons he bred in captivity. But he did not know what caused variation in the first place. The development of the science of genetics has made it possible to understand in much greater detail how variation occurs. It turns out that variation occurs for a variety of reasons.

Every organism has its genome, its genetic identity that is the foundation for how it will develop and relate to its environment. But changes in the genome can occur due to mutations. Mutations occur when the genetic code is not copied exactly. Mutations also can occur due to impacts of external factors such as viruses or chemicals in the environment. Mutations can even occur because bits of the genetic code move within the genome. Whatever the cause, genetic mutations increase genetic variety within a population of organisms.

In sexually reproducing organisms, variety is enhanced by the sharing of genes between the two parents. But even some bacteria, which reproduce by dividing, also conjugate, that is, they share genetic material between them, again increasing genetic variety.

Variety also can occur due to larger scale factors like genetic drift. Migration also can separate populations from one another. The frequency of genomes in separated populations is unlikely to be identical. This creates a divergent genetic base on which the processes of natural selection can operate.

Stephen Jay Gould (1941–2002): American paleontologist Stephen Jay Gould was a scientist who wrote about evolution for the general public. Along with his fellow scientist, Niles Eldridge, he developed the "punctuated equilibrium" model of biological evolution. For them the fossil record showed long periods of species stability "punctuated" with periods of rapid species change.

It was in response to Pope John Paul II's October 1996 address on evolution to the Pontifical Academy of Science that Gould wrote an article, "Non-overlapping Magisteria," in the magazine *Natural History* in which he declared:

"The lack of conflict between science and religion arises from a lack of overlap between their respective domains of professional expertise–science in the empirical constitution of the universe and religion in the search for proper ethical value and the spiritual meaning of our lives."

He further elaborated this idea of "non-overlapping magisteria" in his book, *Rocks of Ages: Science and Religion in the Fullness of Life* (2002).

Hominins: This is the designation commonly used to refer to *Homo sapiens* and all prior related species since the evolutionary branching from our common ancestor with chimpanzees and bonobos. "Hominids" is the term used to refer to all those species that derived from the common ancestor of orangutans, gorillas, chimpanzees, bonobos, and the hominins.

Immanuel Kant (1724–1804): Although primarily known as a philosopher, Immanuel Kant wrote on many subjects, including astronomy. He proposed a "nebular hypothesis" for the formation of the solar system in which the Sun and planets condensed from a swirling cloud of interstellar dust.

With respect to knowledge, Kant reinforced the division of reality separating reason from faith, object from subject, and facts from values in his major works: *Critique of Pure Reason* (1781), the *Critique of Practical Reason* (1788), and the *Critique of Judgment* (1790).

Natural selection: Genetic variation occurs in individuals, but evolution occurs in populations. The interactions between genetic variations among individuals, and the environment in which the population exists, result in changes in the frequency of genes in the population. Individuals bearing particular genes have greater reproductive success because the features related to those genes provide a survival advantage given the conditions in the environment. As a consequence, the frequency of those genes increases in the population. This is the process of natural selection.

Pope John Paul II (1920–2005): In October 1996, in an address to the Pontifi cal Academy of Sciences, the Pope stated the following:

"Today, more than a half century after the appearance of that encyclical [*Humani Generis,* 1950], some new findings lead us toward the recognition of evolution as more than an hypothesis. In fact it is remarkable that this theory has had progressively greater influence on the spirit of researchers, following a series of discoveries in different scholarly disciplines. The convergence in the results of these independent studies—which was neither planned nor sought—constitutes in itself a significant argument in favor of the theory."

However, when it came to the origin of humankind, the Pope held that sci-ence was insuffi cient to account for humanity. He wrote:

"With man, we find ourselves facing a different ontological order—an onto-logical leap, we could say. But in posing such a great ontological discontinuity, are we not breaking up the physical continuity which seems to be the main line of research about evolution in the fields of physics and chemistry? An appreci-ation for the different methods used in different fields of scholarship allows us to bring together two points of view which at first might seem irreconcilable. The sciences of observation describe and measure, with ever greater preci-sion, the many manifestations of life, and write them down along the time line. The moment of passage into the spiritual realm is not something that can be observed in this way—although we can nevertheless discern, through exper-imental research, a series of very valuable signs of what is specifically human life. But the experience of metaphysical knowledge, of self-consciousness and self-awareness, of moral conscience, of liberty, or of aesthetic and religious experience—these must be analyzed through philosophical reflec-tion, while theology seeks to clarify the ultimate meaning of the Creator's designs."

Thus, while affirming the scientific legitimacy of the theory or theories of evolution, the Pope asserted that there were two separate and nonconflicting accounts of human origins, one scientific, dealing with human materiality, the other metaphysical or theological, dealing with humans as spiritual beings.

The Scopes "Monkey Trial" (1925): In 1925, the Tennessee legislature passed the Butler Act, prohibiting teachers from denying the Bible's account of human origins and from teaching an evolutionary account of human descent from "lower creatures." The recently formed American Civil Liberties Union (ACLU) advertised for a case to test the constitutionality of the law. City and community leaders in Dayton, Tennessee, thought that this would be a way of publicizing the community. They persuaded twenty-four-year-old John T. Scopes, a high school football coach and substitute science teacher, to stand as a violator of the law because the state-assigned biology textbook included a chapter on evolution. It is not certain that Scopes actually taught evolution in his class.

The trial was a media event even more than the Dayton town fathers expected. The defense, provided by the ACLU, included Clarence Darrow, one of the most noted defense attorneys in the United States. On the prosecution side was William Jennings Bryan, three-time candidate for the US presidency, and one of the most prominent orators of the day. Bryan died in his sleep five days after the end of the trial.

Scopes was found guilty but his conviction was overturned on appeal due to a technicality in the judge's instructions to the jury.

Theodicy: This is the "problem of evil." This is not so much about moral evil, but about the pain, suffering, and eventual death all living creatures inevitably endure. How can a benevolent God, who pronounces the creation to be not just "good" but "very good," allow such conditions to exist? The entirety of the Biblical **Book of Job** wrestles with this question. It is an issue for which Christian theologians have never been able to provide an ultimately satisfying resolution.

Lynn Townsend White Jr. (1907–1987): The first creation story in Genesis (Gen. 1:1–2:4a) ends with the divine mandate that humankind is to "subdue" and "have dominion over" all of the rest of life on Earth. Some have argued that this perspective has given warrant to and encouraged unconstrained human exploitation of the Earth. One of the most influential articles expressing this view was by Lynn Townsend White Jr. and published in

Science magazine ["The Historical Roots of Our Ecologic Crisis," Vol 155 (Number 3767), March 10, 1967, pp. 1203–1207].

Alfred North Whitehead (1861–1947): Among the students of Whitehead, a British mathematician and educator, were Bertrand Russell, with whom he co-authored a major work on the foundations of mathematics, *Mathematica Principia*, and Charles Malik, who helped draft the "Universal Declaration of Human Rights." At age sixty-three, Whitehead was invited to join the faculty of Harvard University to teach philosophy. His major work was *Process and Reality* (1929; corrected edition, 1979). His philosophical and theological thought has served as a framework for what has come to be known as "process theology;" a movement among some Christian theologians that assumes and seeks to express a coherence between scientific and religious understandings of nature/creation.

ADDITIONAL RESOURCES

The Science of Human Origins

What Does It Mean to Be Human? Richard Potts (National Geographic, 2010)

Masters of the Planet: The Search for Our Human Origins, Ian Tattersall (Palgrave McMillan, 2013)

Human Evolution: A Very Short Introduction, Bernard Wood (Oxford University Press, 2006)

Science and Christianity

When Science Meets Religion: Enemies, Strangers, or Partners? Ian Barbour (HarperOne, 2000)

The Seven Pillars of Creation: The Bible, Science, and the Ecology of Wonder, William P. Brown (Oxford University Press, 2010)

Quarks, Chaos & Christianity: Questions to Science and Religion, John Polkinghorne (Crossroad Publishing, 2006)

Evolution and Christianity

The Evolution Dialogues: Science, Christianity and the Quest for Understanding, Catherine Baker (American Association for the Advancement of Science, 2006)

Finding Darwin's God: A Scientist's Search for Common Ground Between God and Evolution, Kenneth R. Miller (Harper Perennial, 2007)

Responses to 101 Questions on God and Evolution, John Haught (Paulist Press, 2001)

Origins: Christian Perspectives on Creation, Evolution, and Intelligent Design, Deborah B. Haarsma, Loren D. Haarsma (Faith Alive Christian Resources, 2011)

The Galileo Controversy

Galileo: For Copernicanism and for the Church, Third Edition (Revised and
Extended), Annibale Fantoli (Vatican Observatory, 2003)

The Scopes Trial

*Summer for the Gods: The Scopes Trial and America's Continuing Debate Over
Science and Religion*, Edward Larson (Basic Books, 2006)

Online Resources

Science of Human Origins

Human Origins Program, National Museum of Natural History,
Smithsonian Institution – http://humanorigins.si.edu
Anne and Bernard Spitzer Hall of Human Origins, American Museum
of Natural History – https://www.amnh.org/exhibitions/
permanent-exhibitions/human-origins-and-cultural-halls/
anne-and-bernard-spitzer-hall-of-human-origins
Institute of Human Origins, Arizona State University – https://iho.asu.edu

Science and Religion

Broader Social Impacts Committee, Human Origins Program, National
Museum of Natural History, Smithsonian Institution – http://
humanori-gins.si.edu/about/broader-social-impacts-committee
Counterbalance Foundation – http://www.counterbalance.org
Institute on Religion in an Age of Science – http://www.iras.org/essayscom-
mentary.html
Journey of the Universe – http://www.journeyoftheuniverse.org

Science and Christianity

American Scientific Affiliation – http://network.asa3.org

Biologos Foundation – https://biologos.org

Lutheran (ELCA) Alliance on Faith, Science, and Technology – http://luthscitech.org

Presbyterian (PCUSA) Association on Science, Technology, and the Christian Faith – https://www.pastcf.org

CREDITS

The illustration credits listed below take the following form: Page #, Illustration [credit] – "PD" indicates that the illustration is in the public domain; "FU" indicates fair use.

ix, Campfire [Karen Carr, Smithsonian Institution Human Origins Program] – 2, Conflict [James Miller, original drawing] – 2, Separation [James Miller, original drawing] – 3, Interaction [James Miller, original drawing] – 3, Galileo [PD: Ottavio Leoni (1624)] – 3, Inquisition [PD: Cristiano Banti (1857)] – 3, Scopes [Photo by © Hulton-Deutsch Collection/CORBIS/Corbis via Getty Images] – 3, Scopes Trial [Watson Davis (1925) Smithsonian Institution @ Flickr Commons] – 4, Descartes [PD: Frans Hal (~1649)] – 4, Kant [PD: Unidentified painter (~1790)] – 4, Pope [PD: Uncredited (1993), Public Papers of the Presidents of the United States - Photographic Portfolio–1993 Vol. II] – 4, Gould [cropped from https://whyevolutionistrue.wordpress.com/2011/09/11/stephen-jay-gould] – 5, Augustine [PD: The Four Doctors of the Western Church, Saint Augustine of Hippo attributed to Gerard Seghers (1600-1650)] – 6, Teilhard [Photo from Archives des jésuites de France (1955)] – 6, Einstein [PD: Library of Congress (1947)] – 6, Rolston [PD: Photo taken by Flickr user David Keller] – 7, Haldane [National Portrait Gallery, London] – 8, Whitehead [Photo by © Hulton-Deutsch Collection/CORBIS/Corbis via Getty Images] – 12, Augustine [PD: Saint Augustine by Philippe de Champaigne (1645-1650)] – 12, Luther [PD: Martin Luther by Lucas Cranach the Elder (1529)] – 13, Calvin [PD: John Calvin by Titian (16th century)] – 13, Eden [PD: Adam and Eve in the Garden of Eden by Peter Paul Reubens (1615)] – 14, Eve [PD: Creation of Eve by Michelangelo, Sistine Chapel (1509-1510)] – 15, Naming [PD: Photo of Adam Naming the Animals, mural by Barbara Jones (demolished 2009)] – 15, Aristotle [PD: Cropped from "School of Athens," Raphael (1509)] – 15, Linneaus [PD: Carl von Linné by Alexander Roslin (1775)] – 16, Darwin [PD: Photo by Julia Margaret Cameron (1868)] – 16, Mayr [PD: TheFamousPeople.

com at http://www.jbiol.com/content/8/2/13/figure/F1?highres=y] – 17, Tree [PD: Photo from Darwin's 1837 "B" notebook on Transmutation of Species, page 36] – 17, Salhelanthropus [John Gurche, Human Origins Program, Smithsonian Institution] – 17, Lucy [John Gurche, Human Origins Program, Smithsonian Institution] – 17, P. boisei [John Gurche, Human Origins Program, Smithsonian Institution] – 18, H. erectus [John Gurche, Human Origins Program, Smithsonian Institution] – 18, H. heidelberensis [John Gurche, Human Origins Program, Smithsonian Institution] – 18, H. neanderthalensis [John Gurche, Human Origins Program, Smithsonian Institution] – 18, H. floreiensis [John Gurche, Human Origins Program, Smithsonian Institution] – 18, Manhattan [Copyright: <a href='https://www.123rf.com/profile_sepavo'>sepavo /123RF Stock Photo</a> – 19, Igloo [Copyright: <a href='https://www.123rf.com/profile_smit'>smit / 123RF Stock Photo</a> – 19, Tent [Copyright: <a href='https://www.123rf.com/profile_lkpro'>lkpro / 123RF Stock Photo</a> – 19, Astronaut [PD: NASA] – 19, Space Station [PD: NASA] – 20, People [Digital Vision, Thinkstock Photos] – 24, God [PD: Cropped from Creation of Adam by Michelangelo, Sistine Chapel (1509-1511)] – 24, Aquinas [PD: Sandro Botticelli, 15th or 16th century] – 25, Orca [PD: Southwest Fisheries Science Center, NOAA Fisheries Service Photo: John Durban] – 25, White [PD: Photograph, Imogene Cunningham, Special Collections, F.W. Olin Library, Mills College] – 26, Leakey [Robert I. M. Campbell] – 26, Chimps [PD: original source unknown] – 26, Flakes [Human Origins Program, Smithsonian Institution] – 26, Point [Human Origins Program, Smithsonian Institution] – 27, Hominid Timeline [James Miller, original drawing] – 28, Endocasts [James Di Loreto and Donald E. Hurlbert, Human Origins Program, Smithsonian Institution] – 28, Chimera [Human Origins Program, Smithsonian Institution] – 34, Flowers [PD: Wallpaper from eskipaper.com] – 35, Dyson [PD: Photo taken by Flickr user Jacob Appelbaum] – 35, Carter, [PD: soirce undetermined] – 40, Tennyson [PD: http://www.thehistoryblog.com/archives/23732] – 40, Extinction [MasPix, Alamy Stock Photo] – 41, Job [PD: Ilya Repin, Job and His Friends, 1869. Russian Museum, St. Petersburg] – 41, Crucifixion [PD: Carl Bloch, Christ at the Cross, Museum of National History, Denmark] – 46, Homo sapiens Milestones [James Miller, original drawing] – 48, Rice terraces [PD: Jialiang Gao, Twisted Sifter]

– 48, Manhattan[Copyright: <a href='https://www.123rf.com/profile_rabbit75123'>rabbit75123/123RF Stock Photo</a>/ – 52, Liger [Copyright: <a href='https://www.123rf.com/profile_mcherevan'>mcherevan/123RF Stock Photo</a> – 52, Tiglon [PD: cropped from https://ourplnt.com/hybrid-big-cats/tigon]

Made in the USA
Middletown, DE
27 June 2018